Anne Hutchinson

Discover the Life of a Colonial American

Kieran Walsh

Rourke

Publishing LLC

Vero Beach, Florida 32964

www.rourkepublishing.com

PHOTO CREDITS: page 12 Library of Congress; all other photos ©North Wind Picture Archives

Title Page: *Early houses of the Massachusetts Bay colony*

Editor: Frank Sloan

Cover and page design by Nicola Stratford

Library of Congress Cataloging-in-Publication Data

Walsh, Kieran.
 Anne Hutchinson : / Kieran Walsh.
   p. cm. -- (Discover the life of a colonial American)
 Includes bibliographical references and index.
 ISBN 1-59515-137-0
 1. Hutchinson, Anne Marbury, 1591-1643--Juvenile literature. 2. Puritan women--Massachusetts--Biography--Juvenile literature. 3. Puritans--Massachusetts--Biography--Juvenile literature. 4. Massachusetts--History--Colonial period, ca. 1600-1775--Juvenile literature. 5. Puritans--Massachusetts--History--17th century--Juvenile literature. I. Title. II. Series: Walsh, Kieran. Discover the life of a colonial American.
 F67.H92W35 2004
 973.2'2'092--dc22

                                            2004009678

Printed in the USA

CG/CG

Table of Contents

The Young Anne 5

Marriage 6

Sailing to America 9

Anne's Beliefs 11

A Very Smart Lady 12

War Breaks Out 14

On Trial 16

A Move to Rhode Island 19

A Real Hero 20

Important Dates to Remember 22

Glossary 23

Index 24

Further Reading/Websites to Visit 24

The Young Anne

Anne Hutchinson was born in Lincolnshire, England, in 1591. As a child, her name was Anne Marbury.

Anne's father, Francis, was a **deacon** who openly criticized the Church of England. Francis believed the Church had become corrupt. Because he was **outspoken**, Francis was sometimes put in jail.

People who spoke out against the church were often put in prison.

Marriage

When she was 21, Anne married a man named Will Hutchinson. They eventually had 15 children. As young parents, Anne and Will met a Puritan minister named John Cotton. Cotton's beliefs were very similar to those of Anne's father.

Cotton believed that moving to America would enable his followers to worship freely.

John Cotton

Amazingly, Anne predicted the exact date that they would land— September 18.

A group of Puritans arrive to settle in Massachusetts.

Sailing to America

Anne was fascinated by religion. She studied the Bible and developed her own religious beliefs. Some of these ideas clashed with the views of John Cotton. For a long time, Anne kept these beliefs a secret.

Anne and Will followed John Cotton to America in 1634. Cotton and his followers established their colony in Massachusetts Bay.

Anne's Beliefs

In America Anne started to express herself. One idea Anne spread was that belief in God was enough to guarantee **salvation**. Another belief Anne held was that slavery of Native Americans was **immoral**.

The leaders of the colony, particularly John Cotton, were offended by Anne's teachings. John Cotton told Anne to keep her thoughts to herself.

A Native American is taken as a slave, something Anne thought was wrong.

A Very Smart Lady

At this time women were not considered equal to men. In Puritan society, women were expected to be wives and mothers.

But because Anne was so intelligent other people in the colony were drawn to her.

An artist's idea of a Puritan woman

Anne

began having special meetings at her home to read and discuss the Bible. Both women and men attended these meetings.

A Puritan woman reads her Bible.

War Breaks Out

In 1637, war broke out between colonists and a tribe of Native Americans called the **Pequots**. Some men who were followers of Anne refused to serve in this war. Because of this, the leaders of the Massachusetts Bay Colony decided to take action.

A Pequot advises colonial leaders that war is about to be declared.

On Trial

Anne Hutchinson was put on trial. She was accused of **heresy** and trying to overthrow the government. Governor John Winthrop ordered that Anne should be **banished** from the colony.

John Winthrop

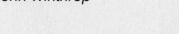

Anne Hutchinson is put on trial for her beliefs.

A Move to Rhode Island

   Banishment was not the end for Anne Hutchinson. In fact, it was more like a fresh start. Along with several of her followers, Anne moved to Rhode Island. There she helped to found colonies at Portsmouth and Newport.

   After her husband died in 1642, Anne moved with her family to New York. In 1643, Native Americans killed Anne and most of her family.

Anne and her family were killed by Native Americans in 1643.

A Remarkable Legacy

On learning of Anne's death, many of the leaders of the Massachusetts Bay Colony were pleased. They thought Anne had gotten what she deserved.

What they didn't see was that Anne was a real hero. At a time when it was dangerous for women to assert themselves, Anne Hutchinson spoke her mind. Her life remains a fine example of genuine religious freedom.

Many Puritan leaders thought Anne's death was justified.

Important Dates to Remember

1591	Born in Lincolnshire, England
1612	Marries Will Hutchinson; meets Puritan minister John Cotton
1634	Follows John Cotton to America
1637	Banished from Massachusetts Bay Colony
1642	Will Hutchinson dies; Anne moves to New York
1643	Anne is murdered by Native Americans

Glossary

banished (BAN ishd) — forced to leave

deacon (DEE kun) — a minister of the church

heresy (HAIR uh see) — opinions that do not agree with established beliefs

immoral (IM mor ul) — wrong or bad

outspoken (aut SPO kun) — unafraid to express opinions

Pequots (PEE qwots) — a Native American tribe in the northeastern United States

salvation (sal VAY shun) — saved from evil or suffering

Index

Church of England   5
Cotton, John   6, 7, 9, 11
Hutchinson, Will   6, 9
Massachusetts   9, 14, 20
Native Americans   11, 14, 19
Newport   19
Pequots   14
Portsmouth   19
Puritan   6
Rhode Island   19
Winthrop, John   16

Further Reading

Bjornlund, Linda D. *The Thirteen Colonies: Massachusetts*. Lucent, 2001
Clark, Beth. *Anne Hutchinson, Religious Leader*. Chelsea House, 2000
Lassieur, Allison. *The Pequots: Native Peoples*. Bridgestone Books, 2001
Stefoff, Rebecca. *Voices from Colonial Life*. Benchmark Books, 2003

Websites to Visit

http://www.infoplease.com/ce6/people/A0824642.html
Infoplease – Anne Hutchinson

http://members.aol.com/ntgen/hrtg/mass.html
History of the Massachusetts Bay Colony

http://www.pequotmuseum.org/
Mashantucket Pequot Museum and Research Center

About the Author

Kieran Walsh is a writer of children's nonfiction books, primarily on historical and social studies topics. Walsh has been involved in the children's book field as editor, proofreader, and illustrator as well as author.